GW00367655

A BOOT UP

DORSET'S JURASSIC COAST

Rodney Legg

HALSGROVE

First published in Great Britain in 2008

Copyright © 2008 Rodney Legg

Front cover: Lulworth Cove © Jason Hawkes

British Library Cataloguing-in-Publication Data
A CIP record for this title is available from the British Library

ISBN 978 184114 687 4

HALSGROVE
Halsgrove House
Ryelands Industrial Estate
Bagley Road, Wellington
Somerset TA21 9PZ
Tel: 01823 653777
Fax: 01823 216796
email: sales@halsgrove.com
website: www.halsgrove.com

Printed and bound by D'Auria Industrie Grafiche Spa, Italy

Contents

How to use this book

The Area

Geology usually comes disguised as scenery but hereabouts it drops the cloak. In 2001 this became the first British natural landscape to win World Heritage Site status. From Exmouth in Devon to Studland in Dorset you can walk through 180 million years of geological exposures in 160 kilometres. The time-scale moves in general terms from west to east, through the Triassic, Jurassic and Cretaceous epochs. Dinosaurs ruled.

The aim of these walks is to sample representative locations, with a bias towards those that have National Trust properties and landform features, ranging from the Chesil Beach and Durdle Door to Old Harry Rocks. Historical and literary mentions abound, from sea and air battles through to shipwrecks and smugglers.

The Routes

All routes are circular — meaning they bring you back to the starting point — and of moderate length. They vary from five to eight miles, and are graded from one to three boots — from easy to more challenging. They are ideal for families or groups of friends looking for an afternoon in glorious countryside or for a more leisurely walk with a suitable pause in one or more of the pubs or refreshment spots en route (except for Tyneham which is on the Army Ranges). None of the terrain is pushchair friendly, so back-pack the toddler.

Starting points are given with both map references and postcodes, because the latter are necessary for some car-borne navigation systems, including that used by an ambulance crew who told me they were 15 minutes in arriving at an emergency because no postcode was given. Direction details in brackets specify compass points which, clockwise, are N (north), NNE (north-northeast), NE (northeast), ENE (east-northeast), E (east), ESE (east-southeast), SE (south-east), SSE (south-southeast), S (south), SSW (south-southwest), SW (south-west), WSW (west-southwest), W (west), WNW (west-northwest), NW (northwest) and WNW (west-north-west). The general direction can be assumed to remain the same until another compass point is given. It really is sensible to carry a compass.

Routes are along public rights of way or across access land that was available and designated as such at the time we went to press. Both categories may be subject to change or diversion. Remember that conditions under foot will vary greatly according to the season and the weather.

Parking places are specified, on the assumption that most walkers will arrive by car, but those using public transport will find that all are close to bus stops with the exception of the National Trust viewpoint above Ring-stead Bay. Bus passengers can join that circuit from Osmington by alighting at the turn for Osmington Mills (where parking can be problematic). Timetable enquiries to Traveline on 08706 082608 or website: www.firstgroup.com

You will be occasionally reminded of accidents and dangers. Not only does the seaboard need to be treated with respect but here and there we have to venture on to the roads without the customary protection of our mobile comfort zone. Risk factors are far higher on the tarmac than any country path.

The Maps

Though we give a self-contained potted description of each walk you may need a map or global positioning system to find its parking point. Our sketch maps can only be a rough guide. A detailed map will prove more useful if you stray from the route or are forced to cut the walk short. Remember that practical problems on the day may range from exhaustion to hill fog.

Two Ordnance Survey maps currently cover the entire Dorset coast. These are Explorer 116 (Seaton in Devon to West Bay) and Outdoor Leisure 15 (Burton Bradstock to Studland). For availability, access www.ordnancesurvey.co.uk/leisure

Key to Symbols Used

Level of difficulty:

Easy 🐚

Fair 🐚 🐚

More challenging 🐚 🐚 🐚

Map symbols:

🚗 Park & start

── Tarred Road

- - - Unpaved road

----- Footpath

■ Building

+ Church

▲ Triangulation pillar or other landmark

🚻 WC

🍴 Refreshments

🍺 Pub

Walk Locations

- Shaftesbury
- Sherborne
- Blandford

1 Lyme Regis

2 Bridport

3

4

- Dorchester

6

7 8

Wareham ■

Poole

Christchurch

10

Bournemouth

9 • Swanage

- Weymouth

5 Portland

├ 10 km ┤

1 Lyme Regis

A varied 6-mile circuit sampling just about all aspects of the Jurassic Coast around its most ancient port

Lyme is famously fossiliferous. For evidence that dinosaurs roamed these tropical shores, when our tectonic plate was lying much closer to the equator, you can visit museums local, regional and national.

The Philpot Museum in Bridge Street at Lyme Regis, Bristol City Museum and the National History Museum in South Kensington, tell the Jurassic story through a succession of west Dorset finds. Most have come to light as a result of landslips. These blue lias clays are notoriously unstable. The seascape and undercliff far into Devon was largely shaped by a colossal landslide in 1839, sending 1,000 metres of hilltop into Lyme Bay, and that towards Charmouth turned into the biggest mudflow in

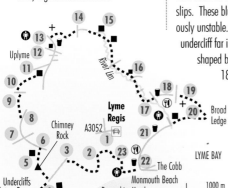

Level:
Length: 6 miles
Terrain: A couple of cliff climbs, but on proper paths provided with steps, otherwise comfortably rural or civilised semi-suburban.
Park & start: In the long-stay Holm Bush car park beside the A3052 in Lyme Regis at the top end of Pound Street, on the south side opposite Coram Tower and the junction with Pound Road.
Start ref: SY 336 920. Postcode DT7 3HX .
Public transport: Good.
Websites: www.lymeregis.com
www.touruk.co.uk

Europe in the winter of 1957–58. One witness of the resultant collapse watched trees marching down the cliff on a mountain of debris that slid out into the sea.

7

Set off: From the opposite end from the entrance, 200 metres away (S), where we are funnelled into Pine Walk, a conifer-lined track between the gardens of houses and bungalows. At the end of the track in 150 metres we turn right (W). Enter the National Trust's **Ware Cliffs** property and turn left in the pasture. Keep close to the clifftop scrubland and cross a small stream in 70 metres. Then enter the next field and climb the slope.

2 The coast path goes through a gate at the top, in 200 metres, on to **Devonshire Head**, which is also Trust-owned. Here we enter Devon. The view to the left is over Monmouth Beach to the famous arc of Lyme's mediaeval Cobb harbour

Alongside the Cobb

projecting into **Lyme Bay**. After badger setts and landslips – minor by Lyme standards – we climb inland to the kissing gates below and facing Clifden bungalow in 250 metres.

3 Turn left (SW) along the tarred road and follow it for 400 metres to the transformer pole and sycamore-covered knolls above **Underhill Farm**. Straight ahead is the **Undercliffs National Nature Reserve**.

4 Here we turn right (N), uphill, along a public path to Ware Lane. Fork right on the slope, in 75 metres, between tall sycamores and a tumble of rocks. In another 75 metres we cross a plank bridge and then scale the steps to the magnificent **Chimney Rock** outcrop.

King Edward I gave Lyme its royal cachet – Lyme Regis – with a charter in 1284.

5 The final steps lead to a stile. We then follow the hedgerow (NW) to **Ware Farm** in 150 metres. Turn right beside the garden and keep it to your left, crossing left of centre to a gap in the hedge and the gate above Ware Lane (NE) in 50 metres.

6 Turn left and walk up the lane (NW) to the main road in 300 metres.

7 Cross over the A3052, into **Gore Lane** (N), which heads towards Uplyme. In 400 metres we pass the turning to Hill Farm House. In a further 125 metres there is a passing place on the left side of the road, with a recessed gateway, and public path.

An historic hole in a Coombe Street wall is said to be Britain's oldest post-box, with its rough-cut timber having both horizontal (for pedestrians) and upright slots (for those on horseback).

8 Here we leave the road and follow the hedge and boundary straight ahead. Then cross to the other side in 150 metres, at the kink in the fence, over the second stile. We are heading to the left of Uplyme.

9 In 200 metres, in the corner of this field on **Horseman's Hill,** we turn right to follow the deep-cut footpath between a field bank and

a crumbling chert wall. Descend the flight of steps beside the garden of No. 1 Cuckoo Hill in 75 metres.

10 Turn left along **Cuckoo Lane** (W), to pass the front of the house, and then turn right, over the stile in 50 metres. There are two paths across this field and ours bears right, diagonally, towards Uplyme church (NE). Stiles take us across the track-bed of the Axminster-Lyme Regis railway in 75 metres.

11 Also bear right on the other side of the disused railway. Walk down to the stream and

'Fossil animal'

the right-hand of the two stiles in 150 metres. Follow the road straight ahead, uphill beside the camp shop, to the entrance of **Hook Farm** caravan camp in 200 metres.

12 Turn left, downhill along Gore Lane (N), into **Uplyme**. Go straight over Venlake at **Crossways** (NE) in 350 metres. Also cross the main street, the B3165, beside the Talbot Arms in 100 metres. Continue along **Church Street** which crosses

Jane Austen (1775-1817) lodged in Lyme in 1803 and 1804, in apartments beside Broad Street, and set her novel 'Persuasion' in the town.

the River Lim and passes a row of three cottages to our right in 200 metres.

13 Turn right after the last cottage, which is Brook Cottage, and follow the drive (E) to Cranbrook and Woody Hyde, then onwards through a carpet of wild garlic. This is the East Devon Way. Pass above an attractive bend in the river which we keep to our right.

14 Cross the road below **Tappers Knapp** in 500 metres. Follow Mill Lane for its 800 metre entirety. Beyond Lindens, Millstream and Honeysuckle Cottage we follow a riverside terrace to the rustic idyll of the **Old Mill** with its thatch and mill-wheel. Keep this to your left as you enter a pasture (SE).

The Old Mill

15 Here we re-enter Dorset. Cross a footbridge and turn left in 200 metres. We are now following waymarks for both the Wessex Ridgeway and the Liberty Trail. Pass a waterfall at **Middle Mill Farm**. Then re-cross the river. In 800 metres we cross Colway Lane at the deep-arched **Horn Bridge**. Continue to follow the riverside path which is now tarred.

16 After **Higher Mill** we cross Woodmead Road in 600 metres, into **Jericho**, and pass Lymbrook Cottages where the river surges around a sharp bend. This leads to Jordan Flats in 400 metres where we continue straight up and over Mill Green and down to Coombe Street in 200 metres.

17 Here we join another scenic section of the riverside path, opposite the **Angel Inn** and to the left of Sherborne Lane, where the River Lim runs at two levels with our path being balanced on a causeway between them. The misleadingly back-dated '774 AD' bridge to the right after Lym Cottages leads to Lepers' Well grotto.

Lyme's nude bathers featured in 'Hydromania' which satirical cartoonist George Cruikshank published in London in 1819.

18 The path returns to Coombe Street in 250 metres, via Town Mill Gallery and Mill Lane, Querns Restaurant and Lyme's Fish Bar.

19 Turn right and then immediately left, up Monmouth Street (E) for 100 metres, to the Old Monmouth Hotel where Oscar Wilde also stayed. Cross **Church Street** to the churchyard and pass fossil seller Mary Anning's grave. In the far corner

in 100 metres we have a superb view of Lyme Bay and Golden Cap.

20 From here, at the end of Long Entry, a path descends from **Church Cliffs** to the beach at **Broad Ledge** (SE) in 100 metres. From here we follow the promenade (W) below Gun Cliff, the Marine Theatre and the **Philpot Museum**. Cross the Lim estuary — known as the

Lyme mayor and mariner Sir George Somers (1554-1611) established Bermuda as a British colony by being shipwrecked there in 1610, while trying to relieve Jamestown settlement in Virginia.

Defence of the realm

Buddle — in 250 metres. In another 50 metres we come to the cannon and anchor beside Rock Point Inn, below Bell Cliff and Broad Street.

(21) Continue straight ahead (SW) along **Marine Parade**. Glance up at the ostentatious 18th-century leadwork of stucco-fronted Library Cottage in 200 metres. In a

further 800 metres we pass the Royal Standard and then reach the road (S) leading to the **Cobb** in 150 metres. This provides an essential 250 metre diversion around its ancient causeways.

(22) Then we return to the Cobb Arms beside **Monmouth Beach** and turn left into Ozone Terrace (W). Turn right on the other side of the bowling green (N) in 250 metres. Walk up to a flight of steps

in 200 metres, beside chalet No. 12, which is called Cobb View. Climb the steps straight uphill into the cliffside scrub.

(23) At the top of the steps we cross a stile into a field on **Ware Cliffs**. This is National Trust land. Turn to your right and then go through the gate. The next gate, on the left, returns us to the car-park in 400 metres.

The Cobb at Lyme

2 **Golden Cap**

A relatively demanding 6-mile circuit through commendably wild National Trust landscape

The surroundings to Golden Cap form a time-warp landscape. Wild and unstable cliffs fringe an inland view that remains uniquely pastoral with dense hedgerows which are more unkempt than you would have seen in Victorian times. Virtually the entire parish of Stanton St Gabriel and much of coastal Seatown, Chideock and Eype belongs to the National Trust. A necklace of seaside fields and hills comprise the 1,974-acre Golden Cap Estate which was acquired in stages between 1961 and 1994. There was an Armada-period signal station on the eastern headland, Thorncombe Beacon, which was given to the nation by playwright Robert Cedric Sherrif (1896-1975) whose iconic works covered both world wars, from 'Journey's End' to the film script for *The Dam Busters*.

Level: 🥾 🥾 🥾
Length: 6 miles
Terrain: Variable, with many potential soggy points, across a landscape prone to landslips. There is also the long ascent of Golden Cap from sea-level to summit. Sea-fret, as the locals call coastal fog, is also liable to descend. That said, you may well find it idyllic.
Park & start: Turn south off the **A35** at the top of **Chideock Hill** into Muddyford Lane between it and the short section of dual-carriageway at Morcombelake and turn left at the junction in 100 metres, then fork right in 400 metres up the slope through Langdon Larches into the National Trust car-park in Langdon Wood.
Start ref: SY 412 930. Postcode DT6 6EP.
Public transport: Reasonable (from Chideock Hill).
Websites: www.nationaltrust.org.uk
www.seatown.ukfossils.co.uk

13

1. Set off the way you came, back down the access road (NW), to the bottom of Langdon Larches in 200 metres. Then turn right, along **Langdon Lane**, which from this point is a double-hedged green lane (S) towards the coast.

2. In 900 metres, after passing Knell Coppice to the left, we turn left into **Pettycrate Lane** and

Looking down on Chideock

follow it towards Chideock (E) for 175 yards. Then fork right, along cherty **Combrey Lane**, downhill (SE) towards Ridge Cliff, on the coast immediately beyond Seatown.

3. Turn right in 450 metres, at the junction after **Sea Hill House**, and follow tarred Seahill Lane (S) for its penultimate 300 metres, into Seatown.

4. Here we turn left beside Golden Cap Stores, into caravan country (E), where we turn right in 100 metres to cross the **River Winniford** over a cobbled packhorse bridge which was restored for the National Trust by the Manpower Services Commission in 1988. Proceed on to Trust-owned

Thorncombe Beacon to Doghouse Hill

coastal grassland on the foothills of **Ridge Cliff** (SE) where we join the cliff path in 200 metres.

5. Here we have options. Firstly, you can explore this section of the National Trust access land, by turning left (E) and upwards,

over Doghouse Hill, to Thorncombe Beacon with its 1588-1988 replica fire-bucket at 155-metres elevation in 1,500 metres.

(6) Secondly, now or at any point en route to **Thorncombe Beacon** - or **Eype's Mouth**

Golden Cap, at 191 metres above sea level, is the highest cliff on the South Coast (being higher than Beachy Head, though without quite the same precipitous drop).

From across the water in Lyme

Hotel 1,300 metres beyond - you can turn around and head the other way (W) along the coast path. Once you have decided on the latter course, keep **Lyme Bay** to your left and head for the main target, Golden Cap, which hopefully lives us to its name in the sunlight.

(7) Drop down to the beach at **Seatown** hamlet, and then resume advancing towards **Golden Cap**, which hopefully lives up to its name in the sunlight. Re-cross the **River Winniford** as it seeps through the shingle to the sea to the left of the **Anchor Inn**. Beyond, up and beyond the landslipped slopes in 200 metres, we enter the next magnificent expanse of National Trust scenery.

(8) For 1,000 metres we cross the pastures that comprise the foothills to Golden Cap. Then we tackle the main ascent, following the steps and stages which skirt the main slope and rise to the top of the gravel plateau, in 300 metres.

Lying beside the Anchor Inn at Seatown is the pebble-encrusted 4.5-metre anchor of the Dutch treasure-ship 'Hope', homeward bound for Amsterdam when she was wrecked and plundered on the Chesil Beach, in January 1749.

'Hope' anchor

(9) Pass Bronze Age burial mounds, the memorial stone, and an **Ordnance Survey triangulation pillar**. The summit of coarse grass, dwarf gorse, bracken and heather looks across Lyme Bay from Portland to Beer Head and Start Point. From here, in 100 metres, the only way is down.

(10) We are heading for Charmouth and Lyme Regis. Zig-zag steps by-pass the landslips of **Kitwells Cliff**. Observe any emergency diversions if cliff-falls or

Ridge Barn from afar

English gentleman Thomas Dare and a fiery Scot, Andrew, Lord Fletcher, landed at Seatown as the first of the Duke of Monmouth's rebels to row ashore, on 11 June 1685, but argued over which of them should commandeer a horse – with the result that Fletcher shot Dare dead and fled to Spain.

mud-flows have opened up. The pastures drop down to a wooded gully, in 800 metres, below St Gabriel's hamlet.

 11 Our route continues straight ahead, across the stream,

and up through the undergrowth to the fields beyond. Keep following the coast path (NW) with the tumbling undercliff of **Broom Cliff** down to your left. In 600 metres the track bends to the left (SW) for 150 metres.

12 On reaching the hedgerow we cross it but then turn right, leaving the coast path, and head inland towards Chardown Hill (NNE). Ridge Barn is across to the left.

No service has taken place in 13th-century St Gabriel's Church since before 1800 though after the Napoleonic Wars it was 'frequently used as a receiving house for smuggled kegs of brandy'.

Having followed the hedgerow for 500 metres we then bear left, across the centre of the field (NW) to the farm track in 400 metres.

13 Turn right along this bridle-way and follow it through **Upcot** (SE) in 200 metres. Turn left along its access road (E) for 75 metres.

14 Here we turn right into the field immediately after the buildings. The public path has been diverted and its new course follows the hedgerow (SE) which we keep to our right for 700 metres.

15 On joining a tarred lane we turn right along it, for 350 metres, into **Stanton St Gabriel**.

Inside the ruined church

Turn left beside the green (E) and pass the ruins of St Gabriel's Church in 150 metres. Beyond it we follow the hedgerow to the end of the field in 350 metres.

16 Go through this gate and then turn right (SE) to keep the field boundary to your right. We are now heading towards the inland side of Golden Cap. In 400 metres, on reaching the wild slope, we turn left and follow its fence (E) into the dip in 300 metres.

17 Cross the pasture to the lower right-hand corner of Black Covert and **Langdon Wood** in 150

A coastal radar station on Cains Folly, between Charmouth and Stanton St Gabriel, was put out of action on 14 May 1942 when it slipped down the cliff in a landslide.

Only a couple of buildings remain but in 1650 there were 23 families living in cottages clustered around the green at Stanton St Gabriel.

metres. Having entered the path along the right-hand side of the trees we then turn immediately left (N) and climb the slope into the wood. Look back for an outstanding view of Lyme Regis and Lyme Bay.

18 Turn right (E) on joining the ride through the pines in 50 metres. Proceed along this forest track for 350 metres, and then follow it around to the left (N), to your car in 600 metres.

3 **BURTON BRADSTOCK**

Simple and reasonably flat 5-mile circuit of scenic cliffs and pastures

Yellow cliffs of Bridport sand, 30-metres high layered with harder rock, rise colourfully and precipitously for a kilometre towards West Bay. Golden, iron-stained limestone characterises the local architecture. The effect is often accentuated by deep blue backdrops of sea and sky. Most of the coastal fields are owned by the National Trust. Burton Bradstock village is delightful.

Level: 🥾 🥾
Length: 5 miles
Terrain: Relatively easy going throughout, with only one series of steps, but rough ground in places.
Park and start: Turn off the **B3157** coast road at the Abbotsbury end of **Burton Bradstock** village, southwards along **Beach Road**, into the car-park on National Trust land beside the **Hive Cafe**.
Start ref: SY 491 889. Postcode DT6 4RF.
Public transport: Reasonable.
Websites: www.burtonbradstock.org.uk
www.campinguk.com

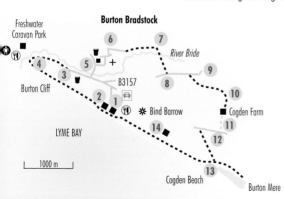

Burton from Southover

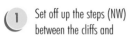

1 Set off up the steps (NW) between the cliffs and **Burton Cliff Hotel**. We follow the cliff path towards Bridport, for the entirety of this section of National Trust land, following the old stone wall beside clumps of purple-flowering thrift and an expanse of coastal grassland. **Lyme Bay** is to your left.

2 Continue straight ahead, along the cliff path, from the turning circle at the end of Cliff Lane in 200 metres. The next stretch of clifftop grass is also owned by the National Trust.

3 In 800 metres we approach the holiday camp and descend to the wide beach where the River Bride trickles through pebbles beside

Freshwater Caravan Camp. Turn right 50 metres after the stile (E) and keep the **River Bride** to your left. Re-enter National Trust land in 200 metres and head across the fields (SE), through gates and stiles, to the tarred road at Southover in 500 metres.

> *Cloth-making was the village trade and net-making – known as 'braiding' – was a cottage industry.*

4 Continue straight ahead, along the road, passing the **Dove Inn**, to Cliff Lane and Cheney's Red House Garage in 250 metres. This is now Burton Bradstock Cars. Here we turn left, into the High Street (N), and cross the **River Bride**. Turn right in

Turning into Mill Street

300 metres, beside the **Three Horseshoes**, into Mill Street (E).

5 This takes us through the village and left beside the site of the former flax mill in 150 metres, to pass **St Mary's Church** in 50 metres (N), and then right in Church Street (E). In just 25 metres we turn left, opposite the church porch, into Darby Lane (N).

6 Proceed to the junction in 150 metres, beside 1777-built

Darby House, and turn right along **Grove Road** (NE). This passes Burton Mill, with its inscription, in 150 metres. From here we continue straight ahead (E) along the riverside footpath. Keep the **River Bride** to your right.

(7) In 600 metres the path emerges beside a road but instead of joining it we turn immediately right (S), to cross an old stone

Golden sand

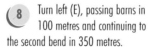

'Mackerel straying' was the shout that had village men and boys streaming down the valley to the sea to set their nets along the beach.

bridge in 50 metres, beside the remains of sluices. Continue straight ahead on the other side, across an arable field and then beside a hedgerow, which brings us to **Bredy Road** in 400 metres.

(8) Turn left (E), passing barns in 100 metres and continuing to the second bend in 350 metres.

(9) Here we turn right, up the slope to the stile beside the gate, and keep close to the left-hand

Fossil finding

side of this grassy field for 350 metres (SE). Go through the boggy gap beside a solitary section of stone wall. Proceed for 75 metres and then turn left, crossing the stream by a stone, up across tussocky grassland to a gateway in the old stone wall on the top of the slope in 150 metres.

(10) Cross the field straight ahead (E) to the gap in the other side in 200 metres. Follow the track

Return to Hive Beach

Dorset's first golf links were established along the clifftop between Burton Bradstock and West Bay in 1891.

along the ridge to the drystone wall in another 200 metres.

11 Bear right on the other side, beside a quarry to your left and the corner of the walls to your right, to the summit of the ridge in 100 metres. Here we turn right (S) and follow the track down and around the barns between **Cogden Farm**, in trees to your right, and Cogden Farm Cottages, on the hill to the left. After leaving the buildings

in 300 metres we follow their driveway to the right-hand of the two exits on to the coast road in another 300 metres.

12 Turn right (W) towards Burton Bradstock. Take care and make sure you face the oncoming traffic. In 300 metres we turn left, through the National Trust parking area (SE), and walk down the track to **Burton Mere** and **Cogden Beach** in 600 metres.

13 Turn right and follow the coast path (NW), with Chesil Beach shingle to your left, to the stile at the extremity of National Trust land in 700 metres. Here we pass through the caravan camp below the **Old Coastguard House**.

14 In 250 metres we re-enter National Trust grassland. **Bind Barrow**, a Bronze Age burial mound, and a 1940-built anti-invasion pillbox are on the hillock to the right. In 500 metres we are back in the car-park beside **Hive Cafe**.

4 Abbotsbury

Quite strenuous 8-mile circuit for free, leaving the Sub-Tropical Gardens and Swannery for another day

To this writer, the view from Abbotsbury Castle is the best in Dorset (and arguably one of the finest in England). Oddly, this favourite walk happens to be the only one in this collection that is described in an anti-clockwise direction. Its sequence opens out better that way round. Down below, the great pebble ridge of the Chesil Beach was created when an immense

Level: 🐾 🐾
Length: 8 miles
Terrain: One stiff climb and plenty of pebbles but ordinary decent countryside in between.
Park and start: From the car-park on the south side of the **B3157**, off Rodden Row, 100 yards west of Swan Inn near the Weymouth end of **Abbotsbury** village.
Start ref: SY 578 852. Postcode DT3 4JL.
Public transport: Reasonable.
Websites: www.abbotsbury.co.uk
www.thedorsetpage.com

surge of water from an inland lake that is now the North Sea, escaped into the Atlantic Ocean 200,000 years ago.

Set off into the village, along Rodden Row (W) and right at the corner into Market Street (NW) to the **Ilchester Arms** in 350 metres. Turn right here, into **Back Street** (E).

 In 175 metres, between terraced No. 3 and Spring

Blind Lane

Cottage, we turn left into **Blind Lane** (NW). Follow this past Copplestone and fork left into the deep-cut hollow way that brings us to the rear of the old Chapel Studio in 150 metres. Here the bridleway swings to the right and heads for the escarpment. Jubilee Coppice is to the right in 150 metres.

 Climb the hill and keep taking left-hand options (five rights of way merge on the slope and summit) until you find yourself walking along the top of the ridge (W) in 800 metres. This is **Wears Hill** and we are heading towards the right-hand inner curve of Lyme Bay with the Chesil Beach to your left. Pass several Bronze Age burial mounds and an underground fall-

Monmouth rebel, traveller and writer Daniel Defoe (1659-1731) described Abbotsbury as 'a town anciently famous for a great monastery and eminent for nothing but ruins'.

out monitoring post of the Royal Observer Corps.

 At the final bridleway gate and stile in 1,800 metres we come to a tarred road.

 Continue straight across and climb the gravel slope on the other side (NW) passing to the right of a replica Armada bucket. Cross the stile into the gorse-covered

Abbotsbury Castle

approaches to **Abbotsbury Castle**. Then go down and over the ditches and banks to enter the windswept Iron Age hill-fort in 150 metres.

6 Walk the length of the southern rampart, on the edge of the escarpment, and then descend from the far corner (W) towards Beer Head — England's most westward chalk cliffs — and Lyme Regis. Continue into the far corner of this pasture, into the triangle formed by the stone wall on the right and the main road to your left in 700 metres.

7 Cross the main road here, on the brow of the hill, to the gate and stile on the other side. We are now entering National Trust land and follow the stone wall, now keeping it to our left. Proceed along the top edge of the scrubby ridge,

Much interviewed and photographed, as a legend in his own lifetime, swanherd Fred Lexter (1902-82) lies beneath the carving of a sleeping swan in the churchyard.

Mediaeval monks established the Swannery on the Fleet lagoon long before 1393 (when swans became royal birds), with what was then a square pond, to provide feast-day meat.

overlooking Labour-in-Vain Farm, which is also Trust-owned. Once again there is a line of a Bronze Age burial mounds, strung along the skyline to your right, and there is freedom to roam across the pastures and scrubby slopes of **Limekiln Hill.** In 1,600 metres we pass a splendidly restored limekiln below the humps and hollows of an extensive quarry.

8 Continue towards the two chalet bungalows to the left of the silhouetted Lookout, on The Knoll, of Coastguard and smuggler associations. Exit in 200 metres at the gate and stile beside the main road. Proceed straight ahead along the verge beside the layby.

9 Then fork left in 100 metres, downhill (SW) along a stony green lane. It gradually bends to the left as it descends into **West Bexington**.

The inshore Chesil Beach Bombing Range was the testing place where inventor Barnes Wallis perfected his bouncing bombs, which were taken to Germany to breach the Eder and Möhne dams in the Ruhr on 17 May 1943.

Famous view

10 In 600 metres, at the bottom end of this perfect smugglers' track, we pass The Moat bungalow and turn right and then immediately left to join the tarred road at Tamarisk Farm. Continue downhill, along the road, and pass the **Manor Hotel**. Seaside suburbia leads to the **Chesil Beach** and **Lyme Bay** in 700 metres.

Two arrivals

(11) Turn left (SE) and join the coast road which is signed as a public road 'Unsuitable for Motors'. In places it shares the shingle with the beach. This is Burton Road which leaves National Trust land in 1,500 metres and passes Greenbanks and the clapper-boarded **Old Coastguards**. In another 1,500 metres we pass '**New Coastguards**' or Castle Hill Cottages.

St Catherine's Chapel, dedicated to the patron saint of spinsters, served as a lookout and seamark and is remarkable in having no wood in its structure apart from the doors.

(12) The road is now tarred and passes Castle Farm and the hilltop remains of **Strangways Castle**. In 600 metres we continue straight ahead, beside the car-park, with **Abbotsbury Gardens** being up the slope to the left. Follow the exotic hedge. In 200 metres, after the car-park, the path crunches through fish-tank sized shingle and in a further 100 metres we follow the 'Swannery' arrow on a milestone. Wartime anti-tank concrete Dragon's Teeth cross the beach to the right.

(13) Go through the bridleway gate and continue to follow the hedge, on a path that becomes firm grass and takes a reassuring course into an inland curve (NE). In 700 metres we leave the bridleway and turn right (SE) along a public

Chapel and church

path that skirts the right-hand base of Chapel Hill which is topped by **St Catherine's Chapel**.

(14) Follow this around (N) to the Swannery access road at Nunnery Grove in 1,000 metres.

(15) Here we turn left (NE), into the village, and pass the

Great Barn in 250 metres. Follow the bend around to the left for 75 metres and then turn right, immediately after the monk's fish-pond, towards the monastic Granary. Turn left in 30 metres, up the slope, towards the 'Abbey Remains'. This is the single gable of an outbuilding, known as Pynion End, in 100 metres.

(16) Beyond it we pass **Abbey House** and enter St Nicholas's churchyard, in 50 metres, where Ham-stone coffins of the abbots are set in and beside the walls. Substantial footings of the Abbey Church can be seen in the grass close to the south side of the parish church. Bear right (E), along the back path for 75 metres, then return to the car-park in 50 metres.

Monks' fish-pond and Great Barn

5 **PORTLAND**

Up, down and along an 8-mile circuit of Dorset's seaside extremity

Chesil Beach

Portland Harbour · **Isle of Portland**

Fortuneswell

Verne Prison

WEYMOUTH BAY

Alleluia Bay

Portland Heights Hotel

Nicodemus Knob

Grove Prison

Clay Ope

Portland Museum

Weston

Church Ope Cove

Freshwater Bay

Pulpit Rock

Lighthouse

PORTLAND BILL

1000 m

Portland stone dominates the streets of central London. What is left in Dorset, after centuries of quarrying, is a pitted and pock-marked offshore peninsula which Thomas Hardy described as the 'Gibraltar of Wessex'. Viewed from the hills of west Dorset the Isle and Royal Manor of Portland, has been likened to a bird's beak that projects into the English Channel. Another analogy is a base-metal brooch that dangles from a chain of golden pebbles. Two centuries after providing 'the King's stone' for rebuilding London following the Great Fire, convict-labour built the breakwaters of Portland Harbour as a 'Harbour of Refuge' for the Royal Navy. Portland's

Level: 🦶 🦶 🦶
Length: 8 miles
Terrain: The only complication arises from one prolonged set of downs and ups (to sea level and then back on to the top of the island). Otherwise you have to do no more than shuffle one leg in front of the other and keep the sea to your left.
Park and start: In the first available public parking space after passing through **Fortuneswell**, on the top of the **Isle of Portland,** by turning left beside **Portland Heights Hotel**, into the 'Viewing Areas' beside Yeates Road.
Start ref: SY 689 731. Postcode DT5 2EN.
Public transport: Frequent.
Websites: www.isleofportland.co.uk
www.portland-port.co.uk

colour is grey which contrasts with mainland greens and whites.

1 Set off along **New Ground** (NE) with the famous view of the Chesil Beach, Fortuneswell and Portland Harbour down to your left. Cross the two bridges of the former stone-carrying Merchants Railway which dates from 1825. Enter Glacis

Chesil Beach view

Verne Prison

after the junction with Verne Hill Road in 500 metres.

2 Follow this for just 50 metres and then turn right as you turn the corner to approach the austere back entrance of the 1860-built fortifications of Verne Citadel which is now **Portland Prison**. Turn right to enter the 1892-dated

High Angle Batteries. Their big guns are gone but the barbettes, rail tracks and underground magazines have been preserved.

3 Exit from the coastal corner (E) of the surrounding hillocks in 250 metres. We are heading towards **Weymouth Bay** (NE) beside the chain-link fence of a communications

On D-Day in June 1944, Portland Harbour was the main springboard for the United States 1st Infantry Division, crossing the Channel for the bloodiest of the Normandy landings, on Omaha Beach.

compound with masts to our left and a quarry to the right.

4 Turn right at the clifftop in 250 metres. We follow the remains of the stone wall (SE). Keep the sea to your left for the entirety of this walk. In 200 metres we descend beside Nicodemus Knob stone-cut sea-mark. Proceed to Incline Road in 400 metres and turn right up it.

5 Turn left after the building at the corner in 200 metres and take a path and then a road through a stone gateway. Follow the cliff-side wall. Razor-wire to the right contains the Young Offenders' Institution which now occupies the Victorian convict establishment at **Grove Prison**. Continue straight ahead along the cliff path at the seaward end of the Grove in 700 metres (S). Follow the edge

Wakeham ammonite

of the exposed plateau between **Yeolands Quarry** and the tumbled undercliff of Shepherds Dinner (SE).

6 In 1,500 metres we emerge from these scrubby badlands, between houses (E), and find ourselves on the main street in **Wakeham**. Turn left (S) and pass thatched Avice's Cottage which is the entrance to **Portland Museum**. In 200 metres we pass beside and beneath **Rufus Castle**, aka Bow and Arrow Castle (E). Then comes a sharp right turn (S)

The key to the popularity of Portland stone is that it is easy to cut and carve but hardens as it oxidises on exposure to the air.

down an awesome flight of steps down to sea-level at **Church Ope Cove** in 200 metres.

(7) Turn right after the first 94 steps for an optional diversion to the ruins of St Andrew's Church, tucked under Pennsylvania Castle in 75 metres. On returning to the main path we continue down another 44 steps. Proceed straight ahead from this point (SW), behind

'T. H. 1844' on the stone pyramid at Portland Bill stands for lighthouse-providers Trinity House (not four-year-old Thomas Hardy) – it is a navigation beacon.

Edwin Lutyens chose Portland stone (from opposite Avice's Cottage in Wakeham) for the national Cenotaph war memorial in Whitehall, in 1920.

the central row of beachhuts, beyond which we go up a rougher cut of steps and hereon follow the yellow footpath arrows which are our reassuring waymarks (S).

(8) In 500 metres, after passing exposed sections of rusty sewer pipes the track bears right to climb inland behind cliffside boulders (NW). Follow a zig-zag path up to **Southwell Road** in 300 metres.

Church Ope Cove

9 Turn left along the road (SW) to pass Cheyne Weare viewpoint and then **Cheyne House** in 600 metres.

10 After the drive to Cheyne House we turn left, towards **Freshwater Bay** (SW), through the

Cave Hole

Portland Lighthouse, completed in 1906, has a 3,370,000 candle-power main lamp visible 28 miles on clear nights, with sequence signature of 4 flashes in 5 seconds then a gap of 15 seconds followed by the next pulse of flashes.

cliffside galleries of disused quarries. We are now heading towards Portland Bill with its Lighthouse being visible almost all the way. En route are **God Nore**, Limekiln Cave, Sand Holes, Cave Hole, **Broad Ope**, Longpoints, Cellar's Ledge and Red Crane. The latter is named for one of the derricks that take pot-boats in and

Lighthouse

out of the water. In 2,000 metres we reach the **Lighthouse.**

11 Hereon, from **Pulpit Rock**, the sea is still to our left but what was south has become north. After a 200 metre exploration of former Beacon Quarry we skirt inland (E) around a geological raised beach, from 200,000 years ago, as the sea level rose during a warm interglacial interlude in the Pleistocene ice age. The exposed shingle lies to the left inside the Ministry of Defence's Test and Evaluation compound as we follow the chain-link fence (E) and then turn beside it (N).

12 Pass the Coastguard Cottages and Lloyd's Cottage signal station in 700 metres. Branscombe Lodge, another former home of Marie Stopes, is the old Higher Lighthouse in another 300 yards. Follow the cliff path beside the top-secret **Underwater Weapons Establishment,**

Henry VIII's Portland Castle is the only intact mediaeval castle in Dorset.

'On the word of a Portland man,' is the oath of the island, signifying that printed words were unnecessary in striking a deal.

of Portland Spy Scandal fame in the 1960s, in 800 metres.

13 In a further 1,000 metres we begin to pass to the left of the main housing estate at **Weston.**

14 Beyond it (NE), in 400 metres, the wide open spaces become constricted into a narrow path beneath the outer wall of **Fort Blacknor**. A Victorian emplacement rises to the right and concrete mountings were used for rocket projectile tests in the 1930s.

15 The cliff path then widens and levels out, in 200 metres, though the terrain becomes rougher. Bower Quarries, Trade Quarries and **Tout Quarries** – now incorporating a Sculpture Park – merge together for the final 1,500 metres along Portland's western edge above the West Weare precipice. Below are **Clay Ope**, **Tar Rocks** and **Alleluia Bay**.

16 We emerge at Priory Corner which is the sharp bend where New Road becomes Priory Road. Turn right, uphill (NE) beside the war memorial and its separate plaque to the HMS *Sidon* submarine tragedy of 1955. Pass **Portland Heights Hotel**, in 200 metres, to return to Yeates Road in a further 50 metres.

6 RINGSTEAD

*Comfortable 5-mile circuit on the edge
of the white cliffs*

Seaside hamlets at Ringstead and Osmington Mills lie across the geological divide between Oxford and Kimmeridge clays to the east and the chalk massif rising to the west. This is White Nothe, or White Nose as clifftop resident Llewelyn Powys insisted on calling it from its snout-like shape. It marks the upper end of a 454-acre tract of National Trust farmland, acquired between 1949 and 1984, which includes most of the slopes between Ringstead and White Nothe and sweeps inland to the foot of Moigns Down.

While on his honeymoon, artist John Constable famously painted the view in the drab direction, towards Weymouth and the clay rather than Lulworth and the chalk.

Level: ♥

Length: 5 miles

Terrain: Gentle, with only moderate ascents, on well marked and easy to follow paths. Only a few stiles to contend with.

Park and start: Turn south from the **A353** at **Upton** and then continuing straight ahead from the hilltop junction above Ringstead, in 1,500 metres, to cross a cattle-grid in a further 1,000 metres, into a **National Trust car-park**. **Start ref:** SY 757 825. Postcode DT2 8NJ.

Public transport: Reasonable (via Osmington).

Websites: www.dorsetforyou.com
www.hiddendorset.org

The oil-rich shales have been known to self-combust as at Holworth which has a Burning Cliff.

Map:

From A353 — Upton — National Trust Car Park — 9 — 8 — 7 — Osmington Mills — 6 — Ringstead — 5 — 2 — Sea Barn — 4 — 3 — Whitenothe Cottages — RINGSTEAD BAY — Burning Cliff — White Nothe — Bran Point — Perry Ledge — 1000 m

White Nothe

1 Proceed along the **Ridge-way**, which becomes a stony track (SE). In 800 metres an access road from Holworth comes up from the left and then turns right, in 100 metres.

2 Continue straight ahead from this point, along the bridle-way that is the access track to **Whitenothe Cottages** on the great chalk headland of **White Nothe**. Follow the track to **Sea**

A precipitous path at White Nothe gave arms dealer and author John Meade Falkner (1858-1932) a dramatic escape setting for the hero of his smuggling novel 'Moonfleet'.

Mediaeval Ringstead is a deserted village, with banks and ditches across the coastal plain, and an ancient church (first mentioned in 1227) which has been converted into Glebe Cottage.

Barn, in 250 metres, and bear right (SSE). Cross National Trust access land, to join the cliff path, in another 250 metres.

3 Turn right (NW), above the tumbling undercliff, with **Ringstead Bay** down to your left. Turn left after passing **Holworth House**, in 250 metres, and follow the coast path (WSW). We pass St

Catherine by the Sea and its cliffside graveyard, above Cliff House, in 200 metres. The path then follows a grass strip, to the left of **Rose Cottage**, for 300 metres.

(4) On re-entering National Trust the track becomes wilder as it skirts the overgrown landslip known as **Burning Cliff.** Hereon the descent is through blackthorn scrub to the caravans and chalets at **Ringstead** in 750 metres.

Across Hannah's Ledge

Coastal defence

(5) Bear left, along the shore-line option, to skirt the hamlet (W). Beyond it, in 600 metres, the coast path passes traces of the medi-aeval Ringstead village and then the site of a Cold War communications station, above **Perry Ledge** in 600 metres. Cross the gully at **Bran Point** and continue towards Osmington Mills. The path rises along the cliff edge, below **Upton Fort** in 400 metres (though the fortifications

Smugglers Inn

COAST PATHS
WEYMOUTH 4
OSMINGTON 1

are virtually invisible because they have been set into the contours of the slope).

(6) In 400 metres the path descends to **Hannah's Ledge** and the **Smugglers Inn**, below Goggin's Barrow, at **Osmington Mills**. Having visited the Smugglers Inn we leave it along the inland side but then turn

Graffiti and drawings on the walls of Sea Barn, owned since 1984 by the National Trust, record events surrounding some of the multiple shipwrecks along this shore.

immediately right (E), from the valley road, 250 metres from the shore.

(7) Re-enter the coastal pasture and turn left (N), keeping the Old Coastguard Cottages and other buildings to your left. Enter the compound with the **chalets** in 200 metres. Climb the slope to a stile in 100 metres and join an unpaved road.

During the Cold War, immense steel structures beside Bran Point and Perry Lodge carried the ultra short-wave command and control signals of the United States Air Force in Europe, between Britain and Spain.

Osmington Mills

The most recent of the shipwrecks visible from these cliffs is the steel skeleton on Hannah's Ledge which dates from shortly after the Second World War.

The first mention of the Osmington White Horse, by Thomas Oldfeld Bartlett in his diary entry for 24 August 1808, records that 'an image cut out presenting King George the 3rd on horseback . . . takes up an acre of ground'.

Portland silhouetted

8 Turn left along it, but only for 50 metres, and then fork right at the junction of tracks (NE). Our track passes older chalets and remains of wartime buildings with a view to the left and hillside pasture to the right.

9 In 900 metres we reach the corner of the field and

John Constable (1776-1837) painted 'Osmington Shore, near Weymouth' (hanging in the Louvre) while on honeymoon in 1816 staying at Osmington Vicarage.

the road out of **Upton**. Turn right along it (E) and climb the slope. This is the approach road you drove along earlier. Continue straight ahead in 600 metres (SE). Return to National Trust land, and your car, in 1,000 metres.

7 LULWORTH

Classic 7-mile circuit packed with gems of landform geology

Lulworth, at the heart of Dorset's holiday coast, is world famous. Iconic images of its Cove and nearby Durdle Door are ubiquitous from advertisements and calendars to films and postcards. Vignettes are scattered through English literature. Stand on the cliffs at Stair Hole you are likely to hear a geological lecture as school-kids gather beside

what the textbooks call 'classic exposures'. Limestone rocks form the first line of the coast's natural defences. Then comes a colourful pocket of soft Wealden sands. Inland is a mass of chalk. A continuous belt of coastal downland has a general right of public access for air and exercise from Ringstead in the west to Pepler's Point

Level: 🥾🥾🥾
Length: 7 miles
Terrain: One stiff climb but otherwise undemanding, along paths that are well-marked and generally dry.
Park and start: In the layby beside Holy Trinity parish church in **Church Road**, off the **B3090**, at **West Lulworth**.
Start ref: SY 823 807. Postcode BH20 5SG.
Public transport: Good.
Websites: www.jurassiccoast.com
www.lulworth.com

beside Lulworth Cove in the east. It is tempting to stray from rights of way but always exercise care and caution on these precipitous cliffs. Sometimes the grass becomes as slippery as glass.

① Set off downhill (S) to the junction beside Graybank, just beyond the British Legion Club and Store in 300 metres.

② Turn right and cross to the raised pavement behind a hedge. Follow it, beside Main Road, into **Lulworth Cove** hamlet in 500 metres. Pass Cromwell House Hotel,

Pacifist philosopher and mathematician Bertrand Russell (1872-1970) brought a succession of female friends to his Newlands Farm love-nest between the wars and bathed in the nude at Stair Hole.

Outer Cove

the **Cove Hotel**, Mill House Hotel and the Coastguard Cottages.

③ In 400 metres we approach the beach with its cafe and slipway. Turn right, just before reach-ing the shore, to cross and climb the coastal grassland (SSW). On reaching the viewpoint, in 150 metres, we turn sharply right (NW) to skirt **Stair Hole** (plural holes, actually) and its mini-cove.

'Smooth Talker'

5 Turn left just four metres beyond these garages (SW) to follow the public path behind the grounds of Stair House. This takes us to the cliff path, towards Weymouth and Portland (NW) with closer views to **Dungy Head** and St Oswald's Bay.

6 Beside Oswald, in 300 metres, we turn inland to a stile in 50 metres, and enter the downland above the car-park. Head towards the white line of the incline path on **Hambury Tout** (N) and join the tourist trail in 200 metres.

4 Turn left on reaching **Britwell Drive** in 300 metres. Walk up it (W) to the garages beyond Stair House and Anchor House in 200 metres.

Napoleon is said to have landed at Lulworth Cove and decided as a result not to invade England.

Below Britwell Drive

Man o' War Cove

Turn left along it (NW) up and around **St Oswald's Bay** in 900 metres.

7 Beyond **Man o' War Cove,** named for the shape of its offshore rocks, we come to the **Durdle Door** promontory in 300

metres. Steps lead down to the shingle beach facing the rock arch.

8 Our onward route, however, is upwards along the cliff path (W). We pass above Durdle Door, in 400 metres, to a backdrop of the English Channel and Portland off the white cliffs. Next, in another 400 metres, we go down almost to sea-level at **Scratchy Bottom** and then have to ascend the next wave of chalk downland, up and over **Swyre**

Durdle Door, the limestone rock-arch, takes its name from the Old English 'thirl' – meaning 'holed' – because 'th' sounds are pronounced 'd' in the Dorset dialect.

Durdle Door

Head. Offshore are a series of limestone rocks, from the Bull and Blind Cow to the Cow and Calf, with the inshore Butter Rock being a chalk stack. Here, in 600 metres, we pass **Bat's Head** peninsula which is perforated by the natural arch of Bat's Hole.

 In 1,500 metres, after the wide Warren slopes and

Drownings at Lulworth included real-life banker William Baring MP in 1820 and the faked disappearance of fictional Sergeant Frank Troy in the film of Thomas Hardy's Far from the Madding Crowd.

Thomas Hardy drew up plans for rebuilding Lulworth's Holy Trinity Church when he worked for Dorchester architect John Hicks in 1869, and used a thinly disguised 'Lulwind Cove' for fictional incidents and settings.

sea-facing Middle Bottom, we pass the lower of a pair of pyramidal **navigation beacons** which line up to point the way into the main East Ship Channel of Portland Harbour. Below us, a column of cliffside chalk is known as **Fountain Rock** (among a series of coastal features that are yet to be given their names by the Ordnance Survey).

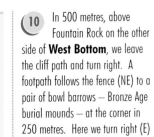 In 500 metres, above Fountain Rock on the other side of **West Bottom**, we leave the cliff path and turn right. A footpath follows the fence (NE) to a pair of bowl barrows – Bronze Age burial mounds – at the corner in 250 metres. Here we turn right (E) to join the **Ridgeway** in 100 metres.

War poet Rupert Brooke (1887-1915) told his mother that West Lulworth was 'the most beautiful place in the world', having discovered it while escaping Bournemouth's 'decrepit and grey-haired invalids'.

11 Continue straight ahead along this track. Follow it and the fence-line, through a succession of fields, for 2,000 metres. Ignore other paths which then branch off towards caravans around Newlands Farm. Our bridleway gradually descends to a grain-store and barns, at **Daggers Gate**, in 1,500 metres.

12 Here we cross the tarred road and continue straight ahead along the untarred public road, uphill (E) to **West Down Farm**, in 900 metres. Proceed beyond it for 400 metres to a kink in the track which we follow around to the right.

13 Leave the track and keep the **mast** to your left as you

Pepler's Point is named for town planner Sir George Lionel Pepler (1882-1959), who for half a century had his holiday home in the old chapel on the site of the original Bindon Abbey, beside Lulworth Cove.

follow the hedgerow (S) down to West Lulworth village.

14 We emerge in **West Road**, in 800 metres, with Churchfield House being the significant building 80 metres down to the left. Our walk turns the other way (W), to the Victorian church and your vehicle beyond in 250 metres.

Butter Rock and Bat's Head

8 TYNEHAM

Short but tough 5-mile circuit available when the Army's Range Walks are open

Boy-toy territory with the hulks of old tanks and intermittent sight or sound of their present-day successors. This is a live-fire gunnery range, with a network of paths that are only open when firing has stopped though you may still see 'dry' military activity (the non-firing type). Armoured fighting vehicles are the Tyneham speciality. The landscape, with its ghost village and farms which were evacuated during the Second World War, forms a time-warp landscape that has become the biggest natural wilderness on the South Coast. Flora and wildlife lists exceed anything recorded on officially designated nature

Level: 🥾 🥾 🥾
Length: 5 miles
Terrain: Strenuous, with rank grass and stiff climbs. Observe danger signs. Stay beside or between the yellow safe-area marker posts for the entirety of the walk.
Park and start: Whiteway View Point on **Povington Hill** which is at the top of the Purbeck Hills midway between **East Lulworth** and **Steeple**.
Start ref: SY 888 811. Postcode BH20.
Public transport: None.
Websites: www.dorsetcoast.com
www.mod.uk

reserves. Note that the paths are open most weekends, at Easter, during block-leave in August, and from Christmas to New Year's Day.

from East Lulworth
from Steeple
Flower's Barrow
Arish Mell
WORBARROW BAY
Gwyle Stream
Tyneham
Worbarrow
Worbarrow Tout
Pondfield Cove
Gad Cliff
Tyneham Cap
BRANDY BAY
Whiteway View Point

1000 m

1. Set off west, through the gate beneath red flag No. 29, beside information boards and warning signs. We are heading towards Portland with the ghost village of Tyneham down in the valley to the left.

'Follow yellow markers'

2. Turn left in 750 metres, in the dip, beside red flag No. 21. The flinty track (SW) descends for 400 metres and then turns (S) for 600 metres to intact St Mary's parish church and the School museum among the ruins of **Tyneham** village. Divert to explore 400 metres of paths.

3. Our onward route is straight ahead (S), following the road through the car-park, for 250 metres. Cross the bridge over the woodland stream and proceed to the corner in 50 metres.

Red flags fly over Tyneham all the time (not just when gunnery takes place) and so-called 'targets' are actually military bearing pickets (direction indicators) for range-finding purposes.

Ghost village

Gad Cliff and Worbarrow Bay

'Comrades', an Australian production about the transportation of the Tolpuddle Martyrs, was filmed at Tyneham in 1984 when thatched roofs were put on cottages and a sycamore tree 'moved' by the Army to recreate the historic meeting place.

4 Here we leave the main track and continue (S) over the stile beside the cattle-grid. Fork left in 10 metres (SE) up the path towards the main slope. In 250 metres the track bends right and ascends the incline (SW), to the craggy clifftop in 300 metres, between bearing pickets T7 and T8.

5 This is **Gad Cliff**, with breathtaking views to **Tyneham Cap,** Kimmeridge Bay, and St Alban's Head (E), and **Brandy Bay** and the English Channel directly below (S). Our route is right (W), along the cliff path

towards offshore Portland and the chalk cliffs of **Arish Mell**, Cockpit Head and Bindon Hill.

6 Follow the coast path, which descends the slope of **Gold Down**, to sea-level at **Pondfield**

Brandy Bay

The site of Sea Cottage

Cove in 1,600 metres. There is an optional diversion up **Worbarrow Tout** (SW) to bearing picket T3 on the 55-metre summit. Our onward course is an easier 150 metres (NNE) to the beach in **Worbarrow Bay** beside the site of fisherman Jack Miller's Sea Cottage. Almost all of the former fishing hamlet of **Worbarrow** has been flattened.

The entire 3,003-acre parish of Tyneham was requis-itioned and depopulated six days before Christmas in 1943, on the orders of Churchill's War Cabinet, to train American tank crews for the forthcoming Battle of Normandy.

Bond, the family name in feudal Tyneham, is that of Bond Street and Ian Fleming whose James Bond traced his roots back from Scotland to Dorset.

7 Here we cross a footbridge over the outlet of the **Gwyle stream** and then pass between yellow markers in the fence-line in 15 metres. Now the route is upwards, beside the footings of a clifftop bungalow and a holiday home, in an increasingly demanding climb of 1,000 metres (NW).

8 On top we cross a stile beside a wartime pillbox and

51

Concrete phone-box

A rare K1 Mark 236 concrete telephone kiosk, installed outside Tyneham Post Office in 1929, pre-dates Sir Giles Gilbert Scott's famous cast-iron design.

turn left to enter the outworks of the Iron Age hill-fort of **Flower's Barrow** in 50 metres (N). This then offers an optional diversion (W), at 175 metres above sea level, to see the impressive banks and ditches which were designed for pre-Roman slingstone warfare.

9 Our route, however, is in the other direction (E). The onward track is the **Ridgeway** along the top of the Purbeck Hills. In 700 metres an untarred road rises from the left, after bearing picket H7, from the direction of Lulworth Castle. We continue straight ahead and pass an Ordnance Survey **triangulation pillar** (elevation 185 metres) in 600 metres. In 500 metres the ridgeway

In 1975, when the Government decided to diffuse the Tyneham controversy by providing public access on an unprecedented scale for a military firing range, it was General Sir Roy Redgrave who created the challenging path network that we now enjoy.

drops down into the dip on **Whiteway Hill**

10 Turn right and then immediately left to cross the flinty road over the hill. We finally retrace our steps of earlier in the day to follow the path (E) back to the car-park in 750 metres.

9 **WORTH MATRAVERS**

Easy-going 6-mile circuit of National Trust quarries and cliffs

Purbeck's stone plateau stretches along the southern coast from St Alban's Head to Durlston Head. Mediaeval marble came from veins further inland but the cliffs are pockmarked and literally undermined by later limestone workings. Most of the stone was lowered into boats and taken to Swanage from where it was shipped to London. Empty and windswept, the coastal ridge protects a ribbon of ancient communities, from Worth Matravers to Acton, Langton Matravers and Herston. All but two of the fields we cross are owned by the National Trust, from the Bankes bequest of 1981 plus adjoining additions

Level: 🦋 🦋
Length: 6 miles
Terrain: Generally easy-going with firm, dry paths or close-cropped grassland. A dozen gates and stiles en route. Three significant descents are steep but short. There are also a couple of flights of steps.
Park and start: The village car-park in **Worth Matravers** is on the edge of the village, beside the approach road from **Kingston** and Corfe Castle.
Start ref: SY 974 776. Postcode BH19 3LE.
Public transport: Reasonable.
Websites: www.beerintheevening.com
www.worldheritagecoast.net

between 1996 and 2007. Limestone plants, maritime birds, naval helicopters and Channel shipping.

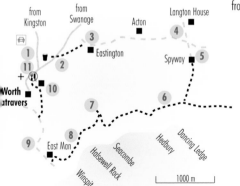

from Kingston
from Swanage
Acton
Langton House
Eastington
Spyway
Worth Matravers
East Man
Seacombe
Halsewell Rock
Hedbury
Dancing Ledge
Winspit

1000 m

Disused underground workings, many protected by gates and grills, provide a refuge for Britain's rarest bats.

1 Set off downhill to **Square and Compass** in 200 metres (S). Here we turn left, along the **Swanage** road (NE), which passes Newfoundland Close. Leave the village in 300 metres and proceed beyond the houses for a further 150 metres.

2 Now turn right, over a stile signed 'Swanage 4', and cross the corner of a pasture (ENE), for 50 metres. This public path crosses a drive and continues straight ahead across the next field.

3 In 200 metres we cross a stile in the hedgerow and are henceforth walking across National Trust land for the remainder of this walk. Keep straight on to the gate on the skyline, in 350 metres, where we join the Priest's Way, which runs between drystone walls (E).

The Square and Compass

Dancing Ledge

4 This bridleway passes **Eastington Farm** and **Acton** hamlet and brings us to a cross-roads of tracks above **Langton House** and Langton Matravers in 1,600 metres.

5 Here we turn right, following arrows to Dancing Ledge (S), between the house and barn at **Spyway** in 200 metres. Continue seawards, up and over the final rise of the stone plateau, to descend to the quarry shelf at **Dancing Ledge** in 1,000 metres.

6 Turn right along the coast path (W), towards St Alban's Head. In 500 metres we pass above **Hedbury** where another of the cliff quarries boasts a Georgian cannon

The Square and Compass pub, named after the key tools of masons and Masonry, was the favourite watering-hole of debauched portrait painter Augustus John (1878-1961).

Shipwrecked cannon at Hedbury

Taking a dip

that was raised from a shipwreck. The much larger quarries at Seacombe come next, in 1,000 metres with galleries three metres high. The steel dome on the slope protected an anti-invasion machine-gunner in 1940.

Jeremiah William Bower (1886-1966), the last quarryman to work the cliffside galleries at Worth, was known as Billy Winspit.

Reflections in the village pond

(7) Follow the path inland (N), but only for 200 metres, to the dense scrub beyond the disused stone workings.

(8) Here we turn left (SW), up steps to the cliff path, which passes more quarries above the **Halsewell Rock** and descends to sea-level at **Winspit** in 1,000 metres. The strip lynchets of **East Man** are up to our right and

Winspit takes its name from a 'whim' or derrick on this cleft in the rocky shore, from which stone was lowered into boats for shipment to Swanage, from 1700 to 1900.

those on **West Man** terrace the opposite slope.

 Turn right in the valley floor (NW), away from the sea and the quarries, and follow the track inland. **Winspit Cottage** is to our right. In 900 metres, after the third bend, we fork right (N). Follow the stream up into **Worth Matravers** village in 500 metres.

10 Cross the stile and follow walls and hedges to the

Keates Quarry, on National Trust land between Worth and Acton, produced the longest set of dinosaur footprints ever found in Britain – discovered in 1997 – from a group of three-toed brachiosaurid sauropods living 145 million years ago.

village green, pond and Post Office, below the parish church of St Nicholas, in 150 metres.

11 Turn right (NE), up to the junction below the **Square and Compass** in 150 metres. The car-park is up to the left (N) in 150 metres.

The eastern cliffs

10 **STUDLAND**

Moderate 5-mile circuit of National Trust coast, downs and heath in the Isle of Purbeck

Sun-worship and public nudity but no fossils. Studland's wide sands were the wartime setting for rehearsing the invasion of Normandy. Across the water, chalk stacks at Old Harry Rocks in Purbeck face the Needles of the Isle of Wight.

Cross-Channel ferries come between them. Enid Blyton sat at the table beside the Isle of Purbeck Golf Club to write her books, from 1951 to 1965, having bought the course as a present for her surgeon husband. Everywhere en route is owned by the National Trust in this easily walkable mix of rights of way,

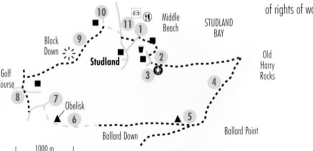

Level: 🥾
Length: 5 miles
Terrain: No difficulties in terms of terrain. Slopes are not overly steep. Summer temperatures may climb – unless fog is rolling in from the sea – and can vary greatly depending on whether you are down in the heath or crossing the 117-metre summit of Ballard Down. There are only four stiles and ten gates to contend with.
Park and start: In **Studland** village at **Middle Beach** car-park, owned by the National Trust, which is at the seaward end of **Beach Road**.
Start ref: SZ 037 828. Postcode BH19 3AT.
Public transport: Good (both from Bournemouth & Swanage).
Websites: www.isleofpurbeck.com
www.nationaltrust.org.uk

permissive paths and access land with a right to roam.

1 Set off south, across the lane, to the path (S) beside the thatched Police post. Go though sycamore trees between Redend Point and paddocks of Studland Manor Hotel. In 200 metres you come to an anti-invasion gun battery, dating from 1940, and much larger **Fort Henry**

Best-selling children's author Enid Blyton (1897-1968) 'always spent her holidays in Swanage', bought the Isle of Purbeck Golf Club for surgeon husband Kenneth Darrell-Waters, and found in Studland policeman Christopher Rone the original 'P.C. Plod'.

Tea on the lawn at Studland Manor

observation post, from which Winston Churchill and King George VI, on 18 April, 1944, watched our own live-fire invasion exercises in **Studland Bay**.

2 In 250 metres turn right, inland (W), away from the

Clifftop memorial to 1944 tragedy

flight of steps that drop down to **South Beach**. Turn left in Manor Road, in 250 metres (S), and pass the **Bankes Arms**. Proceed to public toilets at the bend in 250 metres, facing thatched cottages, in Watery Lane.

(3) Turn left (E) up the track which passes Harry Warren House. Follow the clifftop to **Old**

Fort Henry observation post

Harry Rocks, in 1,500 metres. King Henry VIII's Studland Castle, which stood here, has been entirely washed away.

(4) Continue (SW) along the clifftop, which is known as Old Nick's Ground, above Turf Rick Rock and the Pinnacles. Ascend to the main slope of **Ballard Point** in 1,100 metres.

(5) Here our path curves inland (SW) and climbs to the Ordnance Survey **triangulation pillar** on top of **Ballard Down** in 600 metres. The onward route is along the top of the ridge (W) with views over **Swanage Bay** (S) and Poole Harbour (N). Pass Bronze Age burial mounds and the 1852-dated

Old Harry's Wife – a chalk stack – is still on the map but his original spouse drowned in 1896 in the gale that destroyed Brighton chain-pier.

Judge's Seat which was provided by law writer David Jardine. Marker stones, from 1776, indicate the boundary between Swanage and Studland parishes. In 1,300 metres we cross the site of a wartime radar station.

(6) The next landmark, in 900 metres, is a former gas-lamp **Obelisk** brought from London in 1892. It rises from the side of a prehistoric round barrow. The bridle-

Sea view of Old Harry Rocks

Purbeck used be joined to the Isle of Wight until sea levels rose 30 metres as Ice Age permafrost melted in 12,000 BC.

way continues through the gate and then bends (N) to descend to the road in 500 metres.

 7 Cross the road to the opposite verge and then turn left (W)

along it. Proceed to the stile in the hedgerow at the bend in 250 metres. Turn right (N) and climb up the ridge, through trees on Dean Hill, to the edge of the **Golf Course** in 250 metres. From here we cross the green, following footpath arrows (N), to a stile in the roadside fence, in 150 metres.

8 Turn left (W) along the main road, facing oncoming traffic, to the corner in 50 metres. The track into **Godlingston Heath** enters the National Nature Reserve in 200 metres. Turn right here (E).

Bristol's police-horses come to Studland sands for their summer holiday.

Cliff view of Old Harry

Keep the main heath to your left and that of a heathland restoration project across the hedge and fence to your right, around **Harmony Farm**. Continue straight ahead after the pair of gates and at other path junctions to a branching of the ways in 1,000 metres. Here, just after the mound on **Black Down**, we fork left (NE). Our direction is towards the prominent buildings of Knoll House Hotel.

Studland has the oldest complete church in Dorset with St Nicholas's mix of Saxon and Norman architecture dating from within a few years of King William's Conquest in 1066.

Wartime live ammo is still being found at Studland, so the bomb-disposal team from Bulford Camp calls regularly, to deal with the latest collection.

9 In 500 metres you pass a small covered reservoir, to the left, and come to a gate in a further 225 metres. Proceed straight ahead and bear left at the path junction in 100 metres.

10 Then in 150 metres we come to a cross-roads of tracks at **Wadmore**. Turn right along Wadmore Lane (SE) to the **Ferry Road** in 300 metres.

Bracket fungi on a tree-trunk in Coombe

11 Turn right (S) and head back into Studland village. In 125 metres, after Coombe House, turn left (E) into the Coombe. A public path runs through this wooded glen. Turn left on reaching **Beach Road** in 225 metres. Return to the car-park in 100 metres.